CLASSICAL THEMES

MELODY LINE AND CHORDS
FOR KEYBOARD • GUITAR • VOCAL

HAL•LEONARD®

ISBN 0-634-02079-X

HAL•LEONARD®
CORPORATION
7777 W. BLUEMOUND RD. P.O. BOX 13819 MILWAUKEE, WI 53213

Visit Hal Leonard Online at
www.halleonard.com

Welcome to the PAPERBACK SONGS SERIES.

Do you play piano, guitar, electronic keyboard, sing or play any instrument for that matter? If so, this handy "pocket tune" book is for you.

The concise, one-line music notation consists of:

MELODY, LYRICS & CHORD SYMBOLS

Whether strumming the chords on guitar, "faking" an arrangement on piano/keyboard or singing the lyrics, these fake book style arrangements can be enjoyed at any experience level – hobbyist to professional.

The musical skills necessary to successfully use this book are minimal. If you play guitar and need some help with chords, a basic chord chart is included at the back of the book.

While playing and singing is the first thing that comes to mind when using this book, it can also serve as a compact, comprehensive reference guide.

However you choose to use this PAPERBACK SONGS SERIES book, by all means have fun!

CONTENTS

(contents continued)

(contents continued)

ADAGIO IN G MINOR

By TOMASO ALBINONI

IL BACIO
(The Kiss)

By LUIGI ARDITI

AIR ON THE G STRING
from ORCHESTRAL SUITE NO. 3
By JOHANN SEBASTIAN BACH

ARIOSO

By JOHANN SEBASTIAN BACH

BIST DU BEI MIR

By JOHANN SEBASTIAN BACH

15

BRANDENBURG CONCERTO NO. 2 IN F MAJOR

First Movement Excerpt

By JOHANN SEBASTIAN BACH

FUGUE IN G MINOR
"Little"

By JOHANN SEBASTIAN BACH

JESU, JOY OF
MAN'S DESIRING

By JOHANN SEBASTIAN BACH

1. Je - su, joy of man's de - sir - ing.
2. Through the way where hope is guid - ing.

Ho - ly wis - dom, love most
Hark, what peace - ful mu - sic

20

Word of God, our flesh that
Theirs is beauty's fair - est

fash - ioned
pleas - ure,

With the fire of life im -
Theirs is wis - dom's ho - liest

pas - sioned.
treas - ure.

Striv - ing still to Truth un -
Thou dost ev - er lead Thine

MINUET
from PARTITA NO. 1 IN B-FLAT MAJOR

By JOHANN SEBASTIAN BACH

23

MINUET IN G MAJOR
from the NOTEBOOK FOR ANNA MAGDALENA

By JOHANN SEBASTIAN BACH

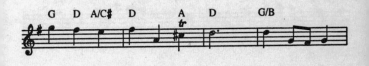

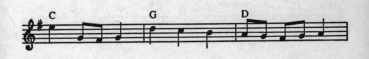

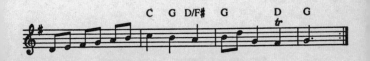

SHEEP MAY SAFELY GRAZE
from CANTATA 208

By JOHANN SEBASTIAN BACH

LES SYLPHES

By G. BACHMANN

FÜR ELISE

By LUDWIG VAN BEETHOVEN

PIANO CONCERTO NO. 5 IN E-FLAT MAJOR

"Emperor"
First Movement Excerpt

By LUDWIG VAN BEETHOVEN

SYMPHONY NO. 5 IN C MINOR

First Movement Excerpt

By LUDWIG VAN BEETHOVEN

35

SYMPHONY NO. 5
IN C MINOR
Second Movement Excerpt

By LUDWIG VAN BEETHOVEN

SYMPHONY NO. 5
IN C MINOR

Third Movement Excerpt

By LUDWIG VAN BEETHOVEN

SYMPHONY NO. 5 IN C MINOR

Fourth Movement Excerpt

By LUDWIG VAN BEETHOVEN

39

SYMPHONY NO. 6 IN F MAJOR
"Pastoral"
First Movement Excerpt

By LUDWIG VAN BEETHOVEN

SYMPHONY NO. 7 IN A MAJOR

First Movement Excerpt

By LUDWIG VAN BEETHOVEN

SYMPHONY NO. 9 IN D MINOR

First Movement Excerpt

By LUDWIG VAN BEETHOVEN

Allegro, ma non troppo, un poco maestoso

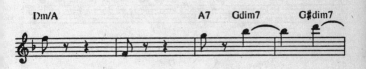

SYMPHONY NO. 9 IN D MINOR

Second Movement Excerpt

By LUDWIG VAN BEETHOVEN

45

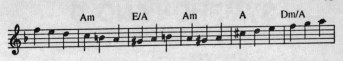

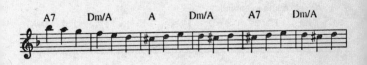

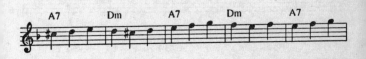

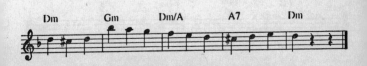

SYMPHONY NO. 9 IN D MINOR

Third Movement Excerpt

By LUDWIG VAN BEETHOVEN

SYMPHONY NO. 9 IN D MINOR

Fourth Movement Excerpt
"Ode to Joy"

Music by LUDWIG VAN BEETHOVEN
Words by HENRY VAN DYKE

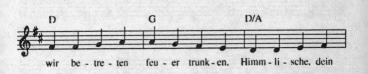

TURKISH MARCH
from THE RUINS OF ATHENS

By LUDWIG VAN BEETHOVEN

CARNIVAL OF VENICE

By JULIUS BENEDICT

RAKOCZY MARCH

By HECTOR BERLIOZ

53

ENTR'ACTE
(for Act III)
from CARMEN

By GEORGES BIZET

FARANDOLE
incidental music from L'ARLÉSIENNE

By GEORGES BIZET

HABAÑERA
from CARMEN
By GEORGES BIZET

OVERTURE TO CARMEN

Excerpt

By GEORGES BIZET

TORÉADOR SONG
from CARMEN

By GEORGES BIZET

Allegro moderato

Fm

Vo- tre toast je peux_ vous le ren - dre. Se-

F7   Bbm

ñors, se - ñors,_ car a- vec les sol - dats,_

Eb7b9   Ab   C7b9   Fm

oui, les to - ré - ros peu-vent s'en-ten - dre:

Ab/C   Eb Ab/C   Ab   Ab/C Eb7   Ab   C7

pour plai - sirs,_ pour plai-sirs, ils ont les_ com-bats!_

Fm

Le _ cir - que_est plein; c'est jour de fê - te! Le

F7   Bb7

cirque est plein _____ du _ haut en bas._

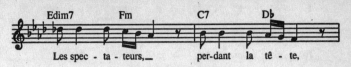

Les spec - ta - teurs,___ per-dant la tê - te,

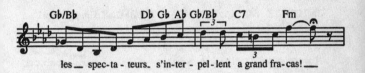

les___ spec-ta-teurs__ s'in-ter-pel-lent a grand fra-cas! ___

A - pos-tro - phes, cris, et ta-pa - ge___

pous - sés___ jus-ques à la fu-reur!___

Car___ c'est___ la fê - te du cou-ra - ge!

C'est la fê - te des gens de coeur! Al-lons! en

gar-de! Al-lons! Al - lons!___ Ah!___

64

To - ré - a-dor, en gar - de!___

To - ré - a-dor!___ To - ré - a-dor!___ Et son-ge bien, oui,

songe en com-bat - tant, ___ qu'un œil noir te re-gar -

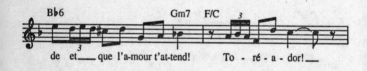

de et ___ que l'a-mour t'at-tend! To - ré - a - dor!___

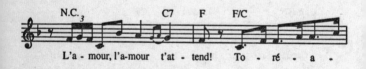

L'a - mour, l'a-mour t'at - tend! To - ré - a -

dor! To - ré - a - dor!___

L'a - mour ___ t'at - tend! ___

WHEN JESUS WEPT

By WILLIAM BILLINGS

When Je - sus wept, _____ the fall - ing tear In mer - cy flowed ___ be - yond all bound; When Je - sus groaned, ___ a trem - bling fear Seized all _____ the guilt - y world _____ a - round.

MINUET
from STRING QUARTET

By LUIGI BOCCHERINI

NOCTURNE
from STRING QUARTET NO. 2 IN D MAJOR

By ALEXANDER BORODIN

POLOVETZIAN DANCES
from PRINCE IGOR
First Theme

By ALEXANDER BORODIN

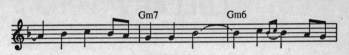

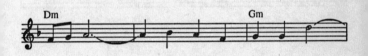

LULLABY
(Cradle Song)

By JOHANNES BRAHMS

PIANO CONCERTO NO. 2 IN B-FLAT MAJOR

First Movement Excerpt

By JOHANNES BRAHMS

SYMPHONY NO. 1 IN C MINOR

First Movement Excerpt

By JOHANNES BRAHMS

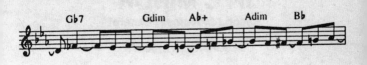

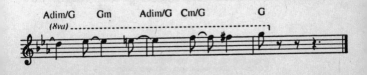

SYMPHONY NO. 1 IN C MINOR

Second Movement Excerpt

By JOHANNES BRAHMS

Andante sostenuto

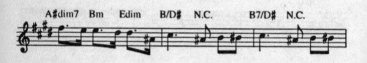

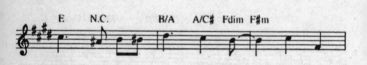

SYMPHONY NO. 1
IN C MINOR
Third Movement Excerpt

By JOHANNES BRAHMS

SYMPHONY NO. 1 IN C MINOR
Fourth Movement Excerpt

By JOHANNES BRAHMS

SYMPHONY NO. 3 IN F MAJOR

First Movement Excerpt

By JOHANNES BRAHMS

SYMPHONY NO. 4 IN E MINOR

First Movement Excerpt

By JOHANNES BRAHMS

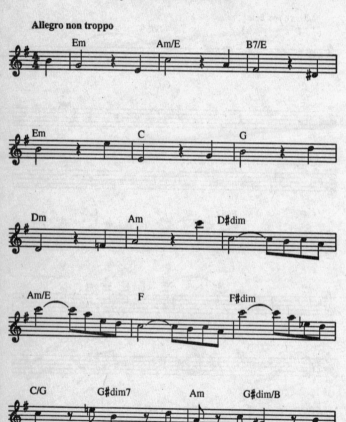

79

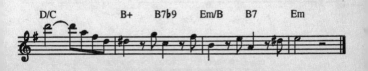

SCARF DANCE

By CECILE CHAMINADE

FUNERAL MARCH

from PIANO SONATA IN B-FLAT MINOR

By FRYDERYK CHOPIN

BALLADE NO. 1
IN G MINOR

By FRYDERYK CHOPIN

PRELUDE IN A MAJOR

By FRYDERYK CHOPIN

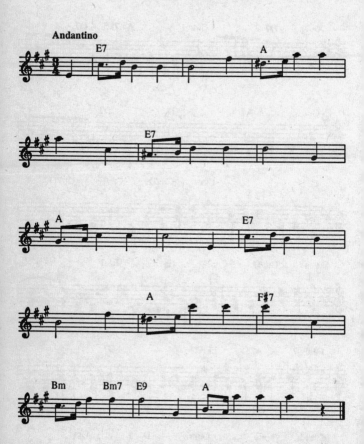

PRELUDE IN E MINOR

By FRYDERYK CHOPIN

WALTZ IN D-FLAT MAJOR
"Minute Waltz"

By FRYDERYK CHOPIN

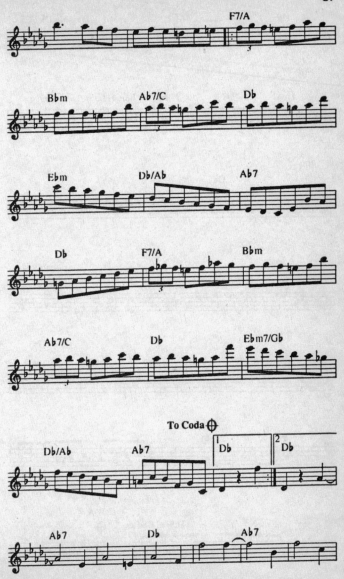

88

TRUMPET VOLUNTARY

By JEREMIAH CLARKE

SANTA LUCIA

By TEODORO COTTRAU

RONDO

By FRANÇOIS COUPERIN

CLAIR DE LUNE

By CLAUDE DEBUSSY

Slowly

LA FILLE AUX CHEVEUX DE LIN
(The Girl with the Flaxen Hair)
from PRELUDES, BOOK 1

By CLAUDE DEBUSSY

RÊVERIE

By CLAUDE DEBUSSY

PAS DES FLEURS
(Dance of the Flowers)

By LÉO DELIBES

PIZZICATO POLKA

By LÉO DELIBES

SYMPHONY NO. 9 IN E MINOR

"From the New World"
Second Movement Excerpt

By ANTONÍN DVOŘÁK

UNA FURTIVA LAGRIMA
from L'ELISIR D'AMORE (THE ELIXIR OF LOVE)

By GAETANO DONIZETTI

Larghetto

U-na fur-ti-va la-gri-ma__ ne-gl'oc-chi suoi__ spun-tò. Quel-le fe-sto-se gio-va-ni in-vi-di-ar__ sem-brò. Che più cer-can-do io vo'? Che più cer-can-do io vo'? M'a-ma. Sì, m'a-ma. Lo ve-do, lo ve-do. Un so-lo i-stan-te i pal-pi-ti del suo bel cor__ sen-

tir! I miei so-spir con - fon - de-re per

po-co a' suoi so-spir! I pal - pi-ti, i pal-pi-ti sen-

tir, con - fon - de-re i miei co' suoi so-spir!

Cie-lo, si può mo - rir; di più non chie-do, non chie -

do. Ah! Cie-lo, si può, si può mo-rir; di più non.

chie-do, non chie

do. Si può mo-rir, si può mo-rir d'a - mour.

THE SORCERER'S APPRENTICE

Excerpt

By PAUL DUKAS

107

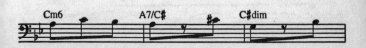

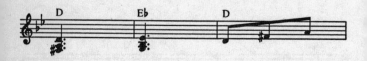

POMP AND CIRCUMSTANCE

By EDWARD ELGAR

PAVANE

By GABRIEL FAURÉ

PIE JESU
from REQUIEM

By GABRIEL FAURÉ

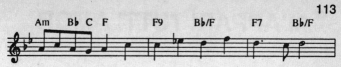

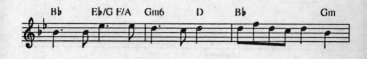

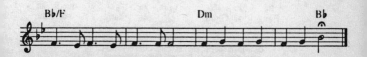

M'APPARÌ TUTT' AMOR
(Ach, so fromm)
from MARTHA

By FRIEDRICH VON FLOTOW

Allegro moderato

M'ap - pa - rì tutt'___ a -
Ach, so___ fromm, ach___ so___

mor, il___ mio squar - do
traut, hat___ mein Au - ge

l'in - con - trò, bel - la___
sie___ er - schaut. Ach, so___

sì che il mi - o cor
mild und___ so___ rein

an - si - o - so a lei vo - lò;
drang ihr Bild___ in's Herz mir ein.

___ mi fe - rì, m'in - va - ghì quell' an -
___ Bang - er Gram, eh' sie kam, hat die

ge - li - ca bel - tà, scul - ta jn cor dal l'a -
Zu - kunft mir um - hüllt; doch mit ihr blüh - te

mor can - cel - lar - si non po - trà, il pen -
mir nue - es Da - sein lust - er - füllt. Weh! Es

sier di po - ter pal - pi - tar con lei d'a -
schwand, was ich fand; ach, mein Glück er - schaut' ich

mor può so - pir il mar - tir che m'af -
kaum bin er - wacht un die Nacht raub - te

fan - na e stra - zia jl cor, e stra - zia jl
mir den sü - ßen Traum, den sü - ßen

cor! _____ M'ap - pa - rì tutt' a -
Traum. _____ Ach, so _____ fromm, Ach, so _____

mor, il _____ mio squar - do l'in - con -
traut, hat _____ mein Au - ge sie _____ er -

116

PANIS ANGELICUS

By CÉSAR FRANCK

Poco lento

(Instrumental)

Pa - nis an - ge - li-cus   fit   pa - nis

ho - mi-num,   Dat   pa - nis   coe - li-cus fi -

ho - mi-num, Dat pa - nis coe - li - cus fi -

gu - ris ter - mi - num. O res mi -

ra - bi-lis man - du - cat Do - mi-num,

Pau - per,_ pau - per, ser - vus et hu - mi -

lis, Pau - per,_ pau - per, ser -

- vus,_ ser - vus et hu - mi - lis. *(Instrumental)*

AVE MARIA

By CHARLES GOUNOD

(based on Prelude in C Major by Johann Sebastian Bach)

tu - i Je - sus. Sanc - ta — Ma - ri - a.

Sanc - ta — Ma - ri - a, — Ma - ri - a, O - ra pro

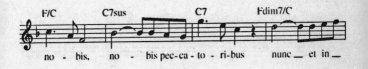

no - bis, no - bis pec-ca - to - ri - bus nunc — et in —

ho - ra, in ho - ra — mor - tis — nos - trae. —

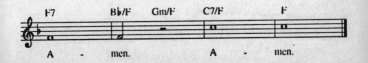

A - men. A - men.

ANITRA'S DANCE

from PEER GYNT

By EDVARD GRIEG

GAVOTTE

By FRANÇOIS-JOSEPH GOSSEC

MORNING
from PEER GYNT

By EDVARD GRIEG

127

IN THE HALL OF THE MOUNTAIN KING

from PEER GYNT

By EDVARD GRIEG

PIANO CONCERTO
IN A MINOR

First Movement Excerpt

By EDVARD GRIEG

AIR
from WATER MUSIC

By GEORGE FRIDERIC HANDEL

LARGO
(Ombra mai fú)
from XERXES

By GEORGE FRIDERIC HANDEL

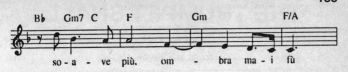

so - a - ve più, om - bra ma - i fù

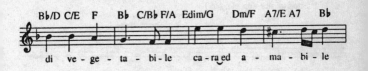

di ve - ge - ta - bi - le ca - ra ed a - ma - bi - le

so - a - ve più, ca - ra ed a - ma - bi - le, om -

- bra ma - i fù di ve - ge - ta - bi - le

ca - ra ed a - ma - bi - le so - a - ve più,

so - a - ve più. (Instrumental)

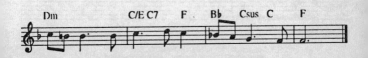

THE TRUMPET SHALL SOUND

from MESSIAH

By GEORGE FRIDERIC HANDEL

Pomposo, ma non allegro

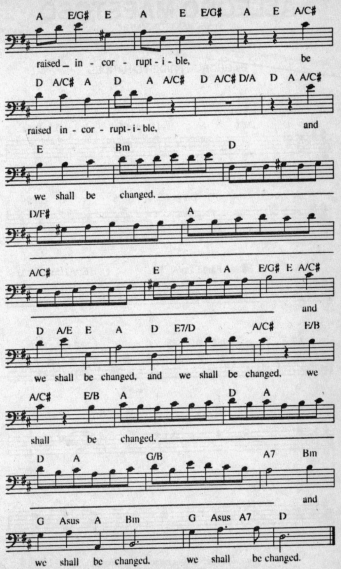

ALLEGRO MAESTOSO
from WATER MUSIC

By GEORGE FRIDERIC HANDEL

SYMPHONY NO. 94 IN G MAJOR
"Surprise"
Second Movement Excerpt

By FRANZ JOSEPH HAYDN

TRUMPET CONCERTO
IN E-FLAT MAJOR

First Movement Excerpt

By FRANZ JOSEPH HAYDN

DANUBE WAVES

By IOSIF IVANOVICI

THE SARDAR'S MARCH
(Cortege du Sardar)

By MIKHAIL IPPOLITOV-IVANOV

THE MERRY WIDOW WALTZ

from THE MERRY WIDOW

By FRANZ LEHÁR

Moderate Waltz

LIEBESTRAUM NO. 3
IN A-FLAT MAJOR

By FRANZ LIZST

TO A WILD ROSE
from WOODLAND SKETCHES

By EDWARD MACDOWELL

EVENING PRAYER
from HANSEL AND GRETEL

By ENGELBERT HUMPERDINCK

SYMPHONY NO. 1 IN D MAJOR
"Titan"
Third Movement Excerpt
By GUSTAV MAHLER

Feierlich und gemessen, ohne zu schleppen

D5

SYMPHONY NO. 5 IN C-SHARP MINOR

Second Movement Excerpt
"Adagietto"

By GUSTAV MAHLER

153

INTERMEZZO
from CAVALLERIA RUSTICANA

By PIETRO MASCAGNI

MEDITATION
from THAÏS

By JULES MASSENET

"FINGAL'S CAVE" OVERTURE
from THE HEBRIDES

By FELIX MENDELSSOHN

SYMPHONY NO. 4 IN A MAJOR
"Italian"
First Movement Excerpt

By FELIX MENDELSSOHN

VIOLIN CONCERTO IN E MINOR

First Movement Excerpt

By FELIX MENDELSSOHN

WEDDING MARCH
from A MIDSUMMER NIGHT'S DREAM

By FELIX MENDELSSOHN

RONDEAU

By JEAN-JOSEPH MOURET

ALLELUIA
from EXSULTATE, JUBILATE

By WOLFGANG AMADEUS MOZART

CONCERTO FOR CLARINET IN B-FLAT MAJOR

Second Movement Excerpt

By WOLFGANG AMADEUS MOZART

SYMPHONY NO. 35
IN D MAJOR
"Haffner"
First Movement Excerpt

By WOLFGANG AMADEUS MOZART

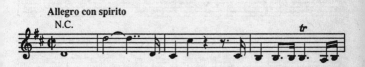

EINE KLEINE NACHTMUSIK

(A Little Night Music)
First Movement Excerpt

By WOLFGANG AMADEUS MOZART

PIANO CONCERTO NO. 21 IN C MAJOR

"Elvira Madigan"
Second Movement Excerpt

By WOLFGANG AMADEUS MOZART

SYMPHONY NO. 40 IN G MINOR
First Movement Excerpt

By WOLFGANG AMADEUS MOZART

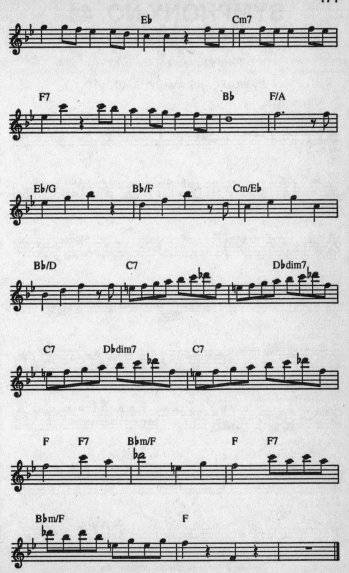

SYMPHONY NO. 41 IN C MAJOR
"Jupiter"
First Movement Excerpt

By WOLFGANG AMADEUS MOZART

TURKISH RONDO
from PIANO SONATA IN A MAJOR, K. 331
Third Movement Excerpt

By WOLFGANG AMADEUS MOZART

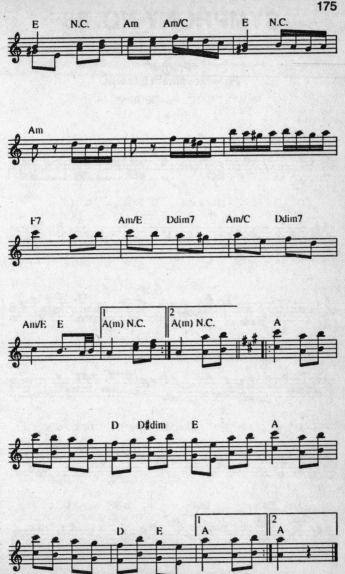

SYMPHONY NO. 38 IN D MAJOR

"Prague"
First Movement Excerpt

By WOLFGANG AMADEUS MOZART

GREAT GATE OF KIEV

from PICTURES AT AN EXHIBITION

By MODESTE MUSSORGSKY

Allegro alla breve, maestoso con grandezza

BARCAROLLE
from THE TALES OF HOFFMANN

By JACQUES OFFENBACH

Moderato

Bel - le nuit, ô nuit d'a-mour, Sou-ris à nos i-vres - ses. Nuit plus dou-ce que le jour, Ô bel - le nuit d'a - mour! Le temps fuit et sans re-tour Em - por-te nos ten-dres - ses! Loin de cet heu-reux sè-jour Le temps fuit sans re-tour! Zé - phirs em - bra-sés,

Ver-sez-nous vos ca - res - ses, Zé - phirs __ em - bra -

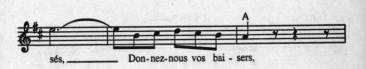

sés, _____ Don-nez-nous vos bai - sers,

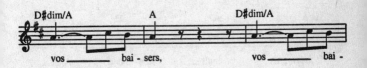

vos _____ bai - sers, vos _____ bai -

sers. Ah! _____ Bel - le nuit, ô

nuit __ d'a-mour, Sou - ris __ à nos i - vres - ses!

Nuit plus dou - ce que __ le jour, Ô bel - le nuit d'a-

mour! Ô bel - le nuit d'a - mour! Ah!

Sou - ris a nos i - vres - ses. Nuit_ d'a -

mour, ___ ô nuit ___ d'a - mour! Ah! __

ah! ___ ah! __ ah! __

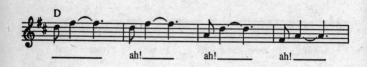

___ ah! ___ ah! ___ ah! ___

ah! ___

CAN CAN
from ORPHEUS IN THE UNDERWORLD
By JACQUES OFFENBACH

MINUET IN G
(Menuet)

By IGNACY JAN PADEREWSKI

QUANDO MEN VO
"Musetta's Waltz"
from LA BOHÈME

By GIACOMO PUCCINI

sia sot - til,___ che da - gl'oc - chi tra - spi - ra;

e dai pa - le - si vez - zi in - ten - der

sa ___ al - le oc - cul - te bel - tá.

Co - sì l'ef - flu - vio del de - dì - o

tut - ta m'ag - gi - ra; fe - li - ce

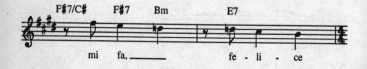

mi fa, ___ fe - li - ce

mi fa! ___

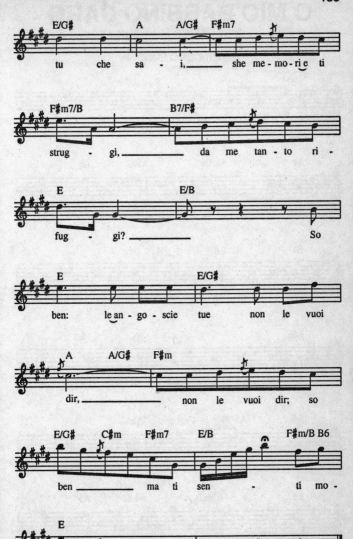

O MIO BABBINO CARO

from GIANNI SCHICCHI

By GIACOMO PUCCINI

O mio bab-bi-no ca-ro,

mi pia-ce,è bel-lo, bel-lo; vo'an-

da — re in Por — ta Ros — sa

a com-pe-rar l'a-nel-lo! Sì,

sì, ci vo-glian-da — re!

E se l'a-mas-si in-dar — no, an-

drei   sul   Pon - te   Vec - chio,

ma per but - tar - mi in Ar - no!   Mi

strug - go e mi   tor - men - to!   O

Di - o,   vor - rei   mo -

rir!

Bab - bo,   pie - tà,   pie - tà! ____

Bab - bo,   pie - tà,   pie - tà!

PIANO CONCERTO NO. 2 IN C MINOR

First Movement Excerpt

By SERGEI RACHMANINOFF

PIANO CONCERTO NO. 2 IN C MINOR

Third Movement Excerpt

By SERGEI RACHMANINOFF

THE FLIGHT OF THE BUMBLEBEE

By NIKOLAY RIMSKY-KORSAKOV

SONG OF INDIA

By NIKOLAY RIMSKY-KORSAKOV

WILLIAM TELL OVERTURE
Excerpt

By GIOACHINO ROSSINI

THE AQUARIUM
from CARNIVAL OF THE ANIMALS

By CAMILLE SAINT-SAËNS

DANSE MACABRE

By CAMILLE SAINT-SAËNS

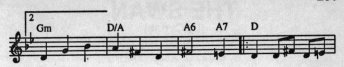

THE SWAN
(Le Cygne)
from CARNIVAL OF THE ANIMALS
By CAMILLE SAINT-SAËNS

Slowly, with expression

TRUMPET TUNE

By HENRY PURCELL

AVE MARIA

By FRANZ SCHUBERT

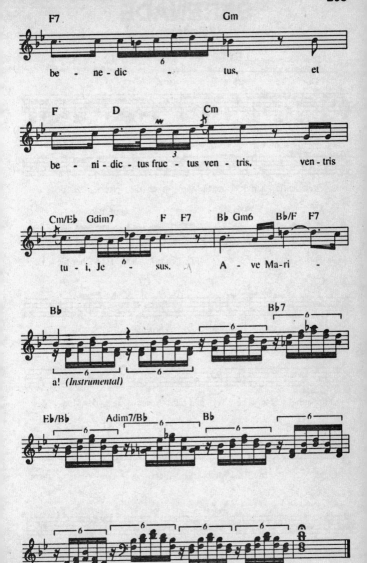

SERENADE
(Ständchen)

By FRANZ SCHUBERT

Lei - se fle - hen mei - ne Lie - der durch die Nacht _ zu dir,

(Instrumental) in _ den stil - len Hain _ her - nie - der.

Lieb - chen, komm _ zu mir. (Instrumental)

Flü - sternd schlan - ke Wi - pfel rau - schen in _ des Mon - des

Licht. in _ des Mon - des Licht, des Ver - rä - thers

feind - lich Lau - schen fürch - te, Hol - de, nicht, fürch - te, Hol - de,

THE HAPPY FARMER RETURNING FROM WORK

from ALBUM FOR THE YOUNG

By ROBERT SCHUMANN

Allegro animato

PIANO CONCERTO
IN A MINOR

First Movement Excerpt

By ROBERT SCHUMANN

FINLANDIA

By JEAN SIBELIUS

STARS AND STRIPES FOREVER

By JOHN PHILIP SOUSA

SEMPER FIDELIS

By JOHN PHILIP SOUSA

216

WASHINGTON POST MARCH

By JOHN PHILIP SOUSA

ARTIST'S LIFE

Excerpt

By JOHANN STRAUSS, JR.

221

BY THE BEAUTIFUL BLUE DANUBE

By JOHANN STRAUSS, JR.

EMPEROR WALTZ

By JOHANN STRAUSS, JR.

225

ROSES FROM THE SOUTH

Excerpt

By JOHANN STRAUSS, JR.

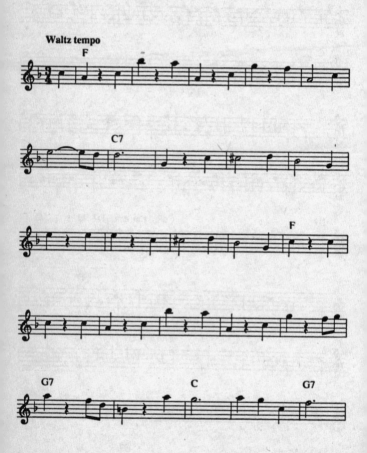

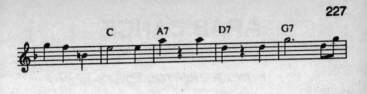

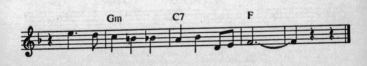

ARAB DANCE
from THE NUTCRACKER

By PYOTR IL'YICH TCHAIKOVSKY

DANCE OF THE
SUGAR PLUM FAIRY
from THE NUTCRACKER

By PYOTR IL'YICH TCHAIKOVSKY

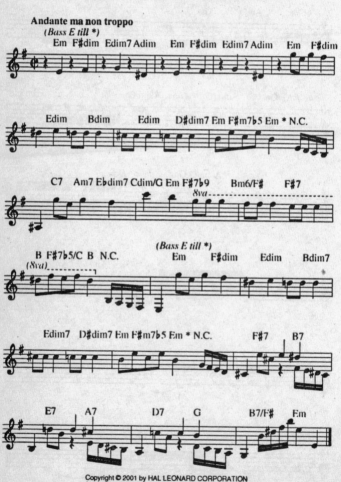

1812 OVERTURE

Excerpt

By PYOTR IL'YICH TCHAIKOVSKY

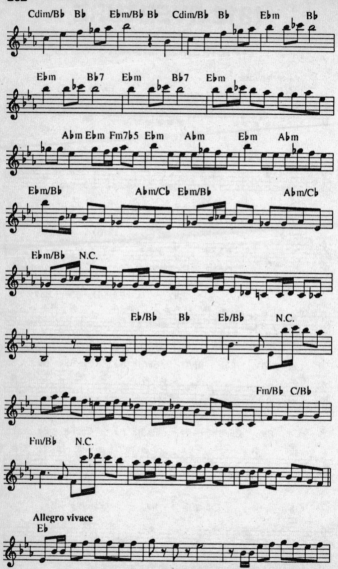

MARCHE SLAV

By PYOTR IL'YICH TCHAIKOVSKY

ROMEO AND JULIET
Fantasy Overture
"Love Theme"

By PYOTR IL'YICH TCHAIKOVSKY

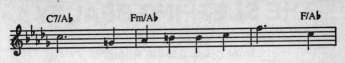

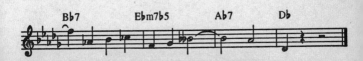

THE SLEEPING BEAUTY
WALTZ
from THE SLEEPING BEAUTY

By PYOTR IL'YICH TCHAIKOVSKY

PIANO CONCERTO NO. 1 IN B-FLAT MINOR

First Movement Excerpt

By PYOTR IL'YICH TCHAIKOVSKY

THEME FROM SWAN LAKE

By PYOTR IL'YICH TCHAIKOVSKY

THE MOLDAU

from the symphonic cycle MÁ VLAST (MY FATHERLAND)

By BEDRICH SMETANA

LA DONNA È MOBILE

from RIGOLETTO

By GIUSEPPE VERDI

TRIUMPHAL MARCH
from AÏDA

By GIUSEPPE VERDI

BRIDAL CHORUS
from LOHENGRIN

By RICHARD WAGNER

THE EVENING STAR

from TANNHÄUSER

By RICHARD WAGNER

GRAND MARCH
from TANNHÄUSER

By RICHARD WAGNER

249

PILGRIMS' CHORUS
from TANNHÄUSER

By RICHARD WAGNER

GUITAR CHORD FRAMES

	C	Cm	C+	C6	Cm6
C					

	C#	C#m	C#+	C#6	C#m6
C#/Db					

	D	Dm	D+	D6	Dm6
D					

	Eb	Ebm	Eb+	Eb6	Ebm6
Eb/D#					

	E	Em	E+	E6	Em6
E					

	F	Fm	F+	F6	Fm6
F					

This guitar chord reference includes 120 commonly used chords. For a more complete guide to guitar chords, see "THE PAPERBACK CHORD BOOK" (HL00702009).

	C7	Cmaj7	Cm7	C7sus	Cdim7
C			3fr		

	C#7	C#maj7	C#m7	C#7sus	C#dim7
C#/Db			4fr		

	D7	Dmaj7	Dm7	D7sus	Ddim7
D					

	Eb7	Ebmaj7	Ebm7	Eb7sus	Ebdim7
Eb/D#		3fr			

	E7	Emaj7	Em7	E7sus	Edim7
E					

	F7	Fmaj7	Fm7	F7sus	Fdim7
F					

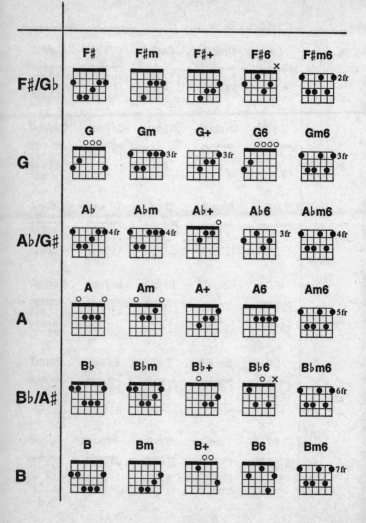

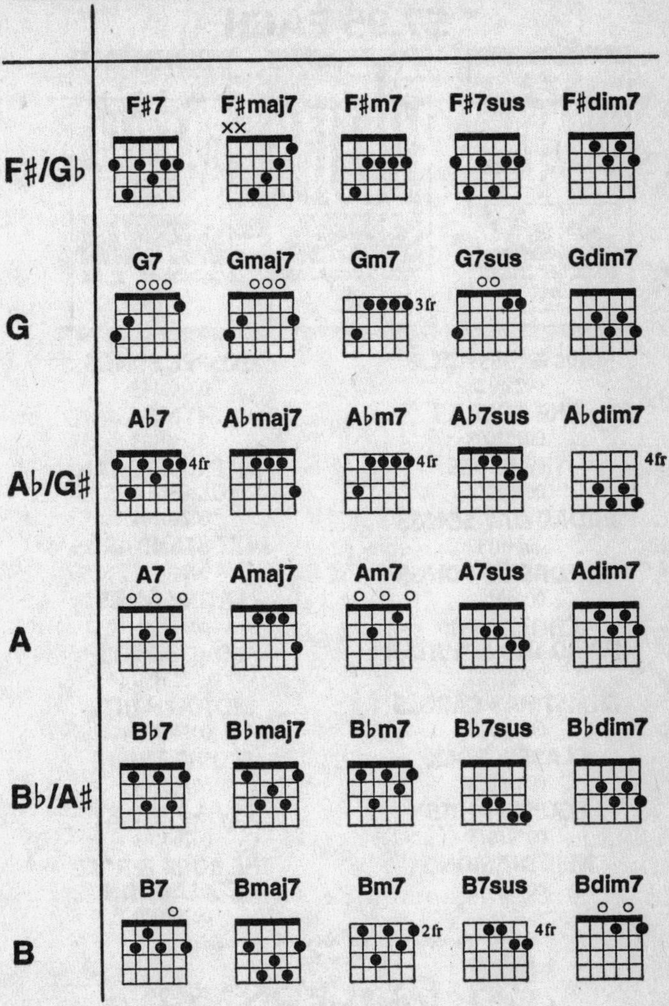
F#/G♭
F#7
F#maj7
F#m7
F#7sus
F#dim7
G
G7
Gmaj7
Gm7
3fr
G7sus
Gdim7
A♭/G#
A♭7
4fr
A♭maj7
A♭m7
4fr
A♭7sus
A♭dim7
4fr
A
A7
Amaj7
Am7
A7sus
Adim7
B♭/A#
B♭7
B♭maj7
B♭m7
B♭7sus
B♭dim7
B
B7
Bmaj7
Bm7
2fr
B7sus
4fr
Bdim7